The Sun Is My Favorite Star

FRANK ASCH

Gulliver Books · Harcourt, Inc.

San Diego   New York   London

Requests for permission to make copies of any part of the work
should be mailed to the following address: Permissions Department,
Harcourt, Inc., 6277 Sea Harbor Drive, Orlando, Florida 32887-6777.

www.harcourt.com

Gulliver Books is a registered trademark of Harcourt, Inc.

Library of Congress Cataloging-in-Publication Data
Asch, Frank.
The sun is my favorite star/by Frank Asch.
p. cm.
"Gulliver Books."
Summary: Celebrates a child's love of the sun and the
wondrous ways in which it helps the earth and the life upon it.
1. Sun—Juvenile literature. [1. Sun] I. Title.
QB521.5.A78 2000
523.7—dc21 98-46383
ISBN 0-15-202127-2

First edition
A C E G H F D B
Printed in Hong Kong

The illustrations in this book were made from black line drawings
and Winsor Newton watercolor swatches painted on Arches 55
medium-grade paper, scanned into a Macintosh G3 computer,
and manipulated with the aid of Adobe Photoshop.
The display type was set in Minister Light and Nuptial Script.
The text type was set in Plantin.
Printed by South China Printing Company, Ltd., Hong Kong
This book was printed on totally chlorine-free Nymolla Matte Art paper.
Production supervision by Pascha Gerlinger
Designed by Lydia D'moch

To Liz

The sun is my favorite star.

In the morning, it comes

to my window and wakes me up.

While I have breakfast, it sends the mist away

and dries up the morning dew.

Then it waits for me to come out and play.

The sun is my favorite star.

Gliding through the trees above my head ...

it follows me everywhere I go.

Its light is bright and hot.

It peeks through a hole in the fence.

It casts my shadow on the wall.

The sun is my favorite star.

Sometimes it plays hide-and-seek with me.

Sometimes it goes away...

…and brings me back a big bouquet.

The sun is my favorite star.

In the evening, it paints

pretty pictures in the sky for me.

Even in the night, it sends

some light to keep me company.

All stars in the sky are beautiful.

But so far…

the sun is my favorite star!